Old Whitburn and Blackburn

with

Longridge and Stoneyb

John Hood

In this view of West Main Street looking east, around 1955, the building on the far left is Christina Archer's long-established newsagent's shop. This family business was started in the 1870s by Daniel and Agnes Archer with the opening of a shop on West Main Street in Armadale. This was followed by two further shops on Armadale's South Street and later by the shop seen here. Later still the business was continued by son John and daughter Mary. Alongside the newsagent's is James Gentles' butcher's shop (under the canopy) and house (with oriel window). In addition to the shop, Mr Gentles had a commercial van (seen here parked in front of the shop) from which he sold his butchermeat throughout the area. To protect the driver and customers from inclement weather, the van was fitted with a roof-mounted sliding canopy.

First Published in the United Kingdom, 2008
Stenlake Publishing Limited
54–58 Mill Square, Catrine, KA5 6RD
www.stenlake.co.uk
ISBN 9781840334173

Acknowledgements

I would like to thank the following people for their help during my research: George Allardyce, Stuart Borrowman, Alister Fisher, Kenneth Livingston, Karen Marr, Joe Murray, and, in particular, Sybil Cavanagh, Local History Librarian, West Lothian Libraries, for her generous assistance during my research, and Bert Gamble and Sybil Cavanagh for commenting on the completed manuscript. I am grateful to Kenneth Livingston for the left-hand picture on page 36, and to Alister Fisher for the right-hand picture on page 36. The publishers gratefully acknowledge West Lothian Local History Library for pictures on pages 21, 31 (inset), 32 and 34.

Further Reading

The books listed below were used by the author during his research. None are available from Stenlake Publishing; please contact your local bookshop or reference library.

S. Cavanagh, *Blackburn: The Story of West Lothian's Cotton and Coal Town*, Edinburgh:
Luath Press (2006).

R. Gamble, *Photographic History of Whitburn*, Blackburn: West Lothian District Council
(2001).

W. F. Hendrie, *Discovering West Lothian*, Edinburgh: John Donald (1986).

The former Longridge United Free Church on Manse Brae, seen here around 1905, was at one time known locally as the 'farmers' kirk', because most of its congregation were farmers. As many of them had to travel quite a distance to get to the church, stabling (for seventeen horses) was supplied. In addition, two pails of drinking water were provided in the porch should any farmer or member of his family wish to quench their thirst. The original church had been established in 1775 as a result of dissatisfaction among members of the several Associate Seceder congregations in the area. It was replaced in 1841 by the building seen here. This church was designed by Lothian-based architect Robert Black in the gothic style, and could accommodate up to 600 worshippers. Although the building has survived largely intact, its distinctive spire has now gone: it was demolished in 1986, because there were insufficient funds to carry out badly needed repairs. The church was closed in May 2000 and has since been converted into flats.

INTRODUCTION

Of the several West Lothian communities covered in this book, the largest is Whitburn, or Whytebourne, as it was once known. Originally an agricultural and weaving community (the former being reflected in the town's coat-of-arms, which has a wheat sheaf incorporated into it), Whitburn greatly benefited from its position at the intersection of two major trade routes: one running east to west (the 'Great Road'), and the other from north to south. When the 'Great Road' was opened in 1795, Whitburn became a regular stopping-off point for the many stagecoaches which ran between Edinburgh and Glasgow. Throughout the 1800s agriculture remained the main occupation in the countryside surrounding Whitburn, while within the burgh itself many were still engaged in the weaving of cloth. By the mid-1800s it was estimated that there were as many as 218 cotton looms in operation in Whitburn itself. As the century advanced, however, and as the weaving industry gradually went into decline, the rapidly developing West Lothian shale-oil and coal industries grew in importance. The extension of the Lothian coalfield and, in particular, the subsequent development of Whitburn's Polkemmet Pit between 1913 and 1922 attracted a new influx of miners into the area and led to the construction of Whitburn's first municipal housing scheme (at Murraysgate). This development was followed by similar schemes at Townhead and Jubilee Road. By the late 1950s, with coal mining in the Lothians in decline, Whitburn and its neighbouring communities combined forces to work on a regeneration project. By far the two most important initiatives emanating from this were, first, an agreement in 1959 with the City of Glasgow Corporation whereby 250 new houses were to be built to accommodate Glasgow's 'overspill' families and, second, the opening of the British Motor Corporation (later British Leyland) truck and tractor plant at nearby Bathgate in 1961. To accommodate this new workforce, the Scottish Special Housing Association built an additional 275 houses in Whitburn.

Originally a fermtoun (the homestead of a farm), Blackburn moved to its present site east of Whitburn in the 1770s, when a local landowner embarked on a series of agricultural improvements, causing villagers to relocate. This 'new town' developed even further when a large cotton mill was opened nearby on the banks of the River Almond in 1793. This in turn led to the setting up of attendant flax, spinning and weaving works. However, by 1840 these works had closed down and, following a fire in the cotton mill in 1877, it was converted into a paper mill. The 1850s saw miners moving into the area to work in the local coal mines, and by the 1880s coal mining had succeeded cotton as Blackburn's principal industry. The opening of the Riddochhill and Whitrigg Collieries in 1891 and 1900 respectively greatly boosted employment opportunities in the area. This in turn led to a large number of houses being built at the west end of the growing town, to accommodate the miners and their families. After the passing of the Addison Act in 1919, the local authority commenced building council houses on the Bathgate Road to cope with Blackburn's increasing population. The first of these new council estates was begun at Riddochhill in 1927 and completed in the 1950s. At that time a start was also made on the new Scottish Special Housing Association housing scheme at Mosside. This housing was required to provide additional accommodation for workers employed in the British Motor Corporation truck and tractor plant in Bathgate. In the 1960s a second major council housing scheme was begun at Murrayfield.

The villages of Longridge and Stoneyburn (which includes Bents) are also featured in this book. Longridge is a farming community which grew up because of its strategic position on the major trade route running south to Lanark. Stoneyburn, on the other hand, owed its development to the sinking of pits at Foulshiels and Loganlea. However, being entirely dependent on this one industry, Stoneyburn suffered greatly when both these pits were closed – Foulshiels in 1957 and Loganlea in 1959.

Although there were still some 1,300 miners employed at Whitrigg Colliery alone in the 1950s, the beginnings of a decline in the mining industry were becoming apparent. In 1968 the Riddochhill Colliery closed, followed in 1972 by the Whitrigg Colliery, leaving Polkemmet Colliery the sole provider of employment in the mining industry in the area. The closure of Polkemmet in 1986, followed soon after by the closure of the British Leyland plant, were major body blows to the economy of the communities covered in this book. Although local authorities have been relatively successful in attracting some new jobs into the area, many residents now have to travel beyond the area for employment.

The village of Longridge, reputedly the highest village in West Lothian, is, as the name implies, built upon a long ridge. While its situation affords excellent all-round views of the surrounding countryside, this also means that the village is exposed to the elements. This is particularly true of Manse Brae on Main Street, where the A706 wends its way sharply downwards towards the neighbouring village of Fauldhouse. Here in wintertime in days gone by the steepness of the brae proved a boon for local children, who would fill pails with water from one of the three cast iron public wells on Main Street and then pour it down Manse Brae to make 'slides' when the water froze. In this view, taken around 1906, the entranceway to the former Longridge United Free Church can be seen on the left. The single-storey cottages on the right of the picture have largely survived to this day. These include Marion (or 'Mirren') Anderson's 'jenny-a-things' shop where, among other things, bread, drapery and sweets could be bought.

These cottages in Cannop Crescent (originally known simply as 1–16 Bents) were built around 1915 by the West Lothian Housing Society, while Bourne End (on the far right of the picture) was erected a few years later. Built specifically for personnel working in nearby Foulshiels and Loganlea Collieries, the cottages seen here in this 1930 photograph still stand (although four others which are out of the picture to the left were demolished in the 1980s and replaced with new private sector housing). The quaintly named Hens Nest Road can be seen on the left. This leads past the former Bents Station to East Mains Farm (known locally as Hens Nest Farm), while the road in the centre of the picture going straight ahead leads to Stoneyburn.

In 1846 a stop known as Bents Station was opened on the North British Railway's Bathgate, Wilsontown, Morningside and Coltness line, to serve the area around Stoneyburn. Although it was mainly for freight, passengers were also catered for. Indeed, pupils from Fauldhouse and Stoneyburn used the line daily to travel to Bathgate for schooling. On 1 May 1930, all the stations on the line were closed to passengers, although goods traffic continued to use the line until 1962. Before the closure of the line, the manning of the level crossing at Bents station was undertaken by Euphemia Mitchell and Jessie Bruce. Working shifts, these two ladies would open and close the level-crossing gates and ensure that the oil lamps, which illuminated the signals at night, were kept trimmed and filled. Although the station booking office (now Station Cottage) has survived, most of the platform and the waiting rooms and signal box were demolished in 1963. Shortly afterwards, the railway line itself was lifted.

Between 1915 and 1917, the West Lothian Housing Society built 58 cottages at Bents. This housing scheme, later named Garden City, was considered to be ahead of its time, in that it provided what was then termed 'low-density' cottage-style housing, rather than 'high-density' tenements. These cottages, some of which are seen here in June 1930, were built for workers at nearby Foulshiels and Loganlea Collieries. Local folklore has it that Manny Shinwell, the well-known Independent Labour Party MP for the County of Linlithgow, once sought refuge in one of the cottages while 'on the run' from the police! However, it is more likely that he was merely afforded hospitality by one of the cottage dwellers when, after losing his constituency seat in 1924 (and therefore without a salary) he was sustained only by fees from a series of poorly paid propaganda meetings. In the 1950s new council housing was built on the open fields opposite the cottages.

The Breich Water, which lies to the south of Bents and Stoneyburn, rises in the former parish of Cambusnethan, before joining the River Almond two miles east of Blackburn. It appears to have been better known locally as the 'staney burn', hence perhaps the origin of the name applied to the village. At one time, Breich Water marked the old county boundary between West and Mid Lothian. However, its historical 'claim to fame' is that on 28 November 1666, a 1,100-strong Covenanting army marching on Edinburgh (on their way to eventual defeat at Rullion Green) forded the river near here – although not necessarily at the partially dismembered stone causeway seen here. I suspect, however, that none of this would be of much interest to the local youngsters in the picture. For them, Breich Water and the surrounding woods were probably somewhere for them to enjoy their own adventures.

Throughout the latter half of the nineteenth century, Bents House (seen here in June 1930) was occupied by local farmer John Elder, who farmed at Bents Farm. By 1912 it was in the hands of his daughter, Miss Helen Elder. Little else is now known of the house or its actual location, as it has long since been demolished. One possibility is that it was situated just to the south of Cannop Crescent, as a 1916 Ordnance Survey map shows what appears to be a substantial property there.

The former miners' cottages at Wilson Terrace (seen here in June 1930) on Main Street, Stoneyburn, were, like the nearby Garden City properties, built around 1915 by the West Lothian Housing Society, which had been established around 1913, with a board of directors representing prominent local citizens. Their stated intention was to provide a better standard of accommodation for the miners and their families. Rather than continuing to erect tenement blocks, which had shared 'privies' and outside wash-houses, they built self-contained cottage-style properties. Each house had a back and front entrance, a back and front garden, an inside bathroom, coal cellar and wash-house. Unlike the tenement blocks which once lined Stoneyburn's Main Street, these cottages have survived, and (externally at least) seem largely unchanged.

Until the local coal deposits were first worked in the late 1700s, Stoneyburn, or Staneyburne as it was then called, consisted of little more than a few small farms. In 1874, however, the Drumpellier Coal Company began working the coal seams on Thomas Maxwell Durham's Foulshiels Estate and, within five years, Maxwell's newly formed Loganlea Coal Company took over the running of this pit. In 1878, in response to a need for housing for miners, Fauldhouse stonemason David Dewar erected four cottages (known locally as Dewar's Buildings) on the soon to be named Main Street. Other cottages, including those seen here in this 1939 photograph, soon followed. Although the housing shown in this photograph has now been demolished, similar properties at Crofthead Row on Burnbrae Road do bear more than a passing resemblance to them.

In this 1930s view of Main Street, Stoneyburn, the Ewing family's long-established Ewington Hotel can be seen on the far left of the picture (with a Morris Cowley saloon parked outside). Immediately beyond the hotel is Strathie Terrace, which was erected by United Collieries Limited for their miners. The houses, which were of the 'room and kitchen' type, were demolished in the mid-1960s. Further along Main Street are the 'Old Rows' or 'Raws', built around 1897 by the Loganlea Coal Company, a mixture of single- and double-storey houses. Like the Terraces, the Old Rows have now been demolished. On the far right of the photograph is White's chemist's shop and, alongside it, the former Stoneyburn Parish Church. Opened in 1925 as a United Free Church, it was closed in 2000 and replaced by the new Breich Valley Church, which was built on the western edge of the village.

This early scene shows one of the many arable and dairy farms which were once a feature of the Whitburn area – there were approximately 50 such farms in 1910. The strength of this farming community was eventually reflected in the existence of an annual Whitburn agricultural show, which ran from 1923 to 1964 and attracted exhibitors from all over the county. Although much of the farms' produce was sold outwith the district, local butter, cheese and milk (both plain and sour) were available for purchase from the several dairies in the town. Since the 1930s many of the small farms have been merged into larger units.

In days gone by, gathering the hay was extremely hard work. It would involve the farm labourers manually raking the hay into small heaps, then piling it into rucks, or haystacks, around a wooden structure which would form their base. The farm labourers seen here are clearly enjoying a welcome picnic – perhaps in celebration of a job well done!

Left: During harvest time in July and August, every opportunity would be taken when the weather was dry to gather in the hay. It was an extremely busy time in the farming calendar and there was an unwritten law that farm workers couldn't take holidays during this time. The two well-dressed farm hands in this photograph are perhaps helping the Stoneyburn farmer, who was reported in the local press of August 1930 as even working on a Sunday to gather in all his hay.

Above: At one time in rural communities such as Whitburn, carters played a vital role in ensuring that produce and livestock found their way to markets, not only locally, but also further afield. Given the isolated location of many farms, and the hilly nature of the surrounding countryside, this was by no means an easy task, especially in wintertime, when it was not uncommon for carters to get stuck in deep snowdrifts.

Until 1620 Polkemmet House was the home of the Shaw family. Thereafter, and for about 300 years, it was the home of the Baillie family of Lanarkshire. Originally built in the Scottish Baronial style, the house was substantially extended in 1822 by Sir William Baillie. During the First World War, Lady Isobel Baillie transformed it into a Red Cross auxiliary hospital, capable of accommodating up to 40 soldiers, and for a time during the Second World War it housed young evacuees. Towards the end of the war, however, it became an 'overflow' hospital for nearby Bangour Hospital, when it was used to house patients suffering from tuberculosis. In September 1945 the Trefoil School for physically handicapped children took over the house, and remained there until 1951 (when the school moved to Gogarbank). At that time (and until 1960) the house was taken over by the Scottish Police College. Polkemmet House was eventually demolished in the early 1960s, with the exception of the stable block and one steading. In 1978 the estate was taken over by West Lothian District Council and it was opened to the public for the first time on 26 June 1981.

The former Lady Baillie School (seen here on West Main Street at the entrance to Bowling Green Road) was established around 1851 by Mary, Lady Baillie, a passionate supporter of local religious and educational causes. In 1885, some twelve years after the establishment of the Torphichen School Board, the 70 pupils then attending the school transferred to Whitburn Public School on East Main Street. At the same time the school playground was torn up and in its place a bowling green was laid (which was opened by Lady Baillie's husband in June 1887). The school was then used for a period as a Sabbath School and by the Whitburn Public Band for practice sessions. In 1923 the building was sold to a local councillor for £238 and converted into a Gospel Hall, which it remains today. Roughcasting now covers the original brickwork; otherwise the exterior remains largely unchanged.

In this 1920s view of West Main Street looking east, open fields stretch in an almost unbroken line. On the opposite side of the road is Murraysgate Crescent council housing scheme, which replaced the old miners' 'rows' that had stood here previously. It was Whitburn's first council housing scheme and was one of five built to fill the need for good-quality housing for the miners coming into the area to work at the newly opened Polkemmet pit. The foundation stone (built into the front wall of numbers 173 and 175) was laid by Provost William Shanks on 7 May 1921.

In this early view of West Main Street looking east towards Whitburn Cross, all of the older buildings on the north side of the street (with the exception of the building on the far left of the photograph) have been demolished, including the adjoining two-storey tenement known as Lawrie's Buildings and the further tenement just to the east of Bog Road. These tenements provided accommodation for miners and their families. When they were demolished, a branch of the West Benhar Co-operative Society (known locally as the 'wee store') was built on the site. At the time this photograph was taken, the area to the west and rear of these properties consisted of farmers' fields, which were often used by local children as a playground. On the opposite side of the street, the area between Bowling Green Road and Murraysgate housing scheme was occupied by the Lady Baillie School and miners' cottages.

In the main, the older properties seen here in the late 1920s, on either side of West Main Street at Smiddy Brae, have been demolished. One exception is the two-storey property on the far left of the picture, the ground floor of which is currently occupied by a hair salon and a florist's shop. The latter was established by Emma Paterson over 40 years ago, when the building was first converted to accommodate two ground-floor shops. Since 1984 the business has been run by Emma's daughter, Jennifer McAuley. During the 1930s, Victor Herd's sweetie shop was one of the businesses in the row of single-storey cottages which adjoined the florist's. As well as being popular with local children, the sweetie shop was also well used by patrons of the picture house (known locally as the 'wee hall'), which was conveniently situated right next door to it. In this area now is the Clachan Bar, a Spar store, a bookmaker's and a new police station.

Whitburn Prize Brass Band (seen here around 1905), formed in 1871, was initially known as Whitburn Town Band. It had another change of name in 1948, when it became the Miners' Welfare Band, and again in 1962, becoming the Whitburn Burgh Band. In 1948 they were placed first in the Fourth Section of the Scottish Brass Band Association Championships. This was followed in 1954 by a first placing in the British Third Section and, in 1963, by promotion to the Scottish Championship Section. To date the band have won at least fourteen Scottish Championship titles and had numerous radio and television appearances. In 1981 the Band swept the board, winning all the Scottish competitions and reaching the final of BBC2's Best of Brass competition. Later that year they were placed third in the National Championships and fourth in the European championships. Further success came in 1991 when the band (by now called the Murray International Whitburn Band) won the British Open Grand Shield Championship.

By 1914 the annual Children's Gala Day procession had become a very popular event. The idea of a Children's Gala Day was first suggested by the Whitburn Town Band in 1907. That year, however, because of inclement weather, the event (which should have included an afternoon of games, followed by refreshments at a local farm) was confined to a parade from Whitburn Public School, along East and West Main Streets to Murraysgate, before returning to the school for refreshments. Undaunted, they held the event the following year and, from 1910 onwards, the parade became more and more of a spectacle, with participants on foot, bicycles, and horse-drawn and motorised floats. In addition houses on Main Street were festooned with banners. In 1911, in celebration of the coronation of King George V and Queen Mary, each child who participated in Gala Day was given a china mug and chocolates. This 1914 photograph shows the procession in West Main Street passing, on the far left, Richard Gibb (plumbers' merchant) and the West Benhar Co-operative Society's Whitburn branch grocery store.

An early and popular addition to the annual Children's Gala Day festivities was a series of massive floral arches mounted at strategic points throughout the town. The first such structure was erected on East Main Street in 1908. The triple arch, seen here before the First World War, was erected on West Main Street and straddled the entire width of the street. Designed and constructed by the miners and their families, these carefully crafted arches, which could be single, double or triple, would take days to complete. For the children, one necessary accessory on Gala Day was their 'tinny' (or tin cup), which they would either carry in their hand or (as with the girl in the black dress with white lace collar) secure over their shoulders with a strap. The 'tinny' could then be used for refreshments (usually milk) which were distributed when the procession arrived at its destination, initially a farmer's field, but in later years the public park.

In this view of Whitburn Cross, taken in April 1928, James Wood & Sons' Yetthouse bakery and confectionery can be seen occupying a prominent site at the corner of West Main Street and Armadale Road. James, who was a native of East Whitburn, established his bakery in 1879. Besides running the business, he also served on the local council for approximately 27 years and was ultimately elected provost. In 1895 he expanded the business, buying all of the two-storey building on this site and adding a tearoom. In the 1980s this property (together with the properties seen on the opposite side of West Main Street) were demolished in order to allow the area at the Cross to be redeveloped. Among the businesses on the south side of the street affected by the redevelopment were William Aitken's newsagent's and confectionery shop, Mrs Bessie Simpson's wool shop and John Murray's ironmongery shop.

During redevelopment in the 1980s all of the older properties seen here on West Main Street, immediately west of Whitburn Cross, were demolished and replaced with modern shop units. Among the businesses affected were James Wood's Yetthouse Bakery and Robert (Bertie) Topping's barber shop. However, on the north side of the street most of the properties beyond the barber's, including the two-storey property known locally as Market Inn Buildings, have survived. From 1723 to the present day, the ground floor of this property has housed the Old Market Inn. For many years on the evening of Gala Day the area in front of Market Inn Buildings was the venue for the popular 'Go As You Please' concerts. As this photograph shows, another popular gathering place was the north-west corner of the Cross. Here, local men would gather to put the world to rights.

In this view, taken from West Main Street, looking east over Whitburn Cross towards East Main Street, the first building visible on the left is Lodge Polkemmet No. 927. The lodge, which was established in 1902, first met in a room in the Town Hall before buying the hall outright in 1924. At that time it was a single-storey building but it was extended upwards in 1929, when the ground floor was enlarged, the walls were raised and the old roof was taken off and reused. Immediately to the east of the lodge are the premises of James Browning's funeral business and car and bus hire company. Almost directly opposite these properties, at the corner of East Main Street and Manse Road, is Davie Morrison's Cross Tavern. The tavern, known locally simply as Morrison's, has occupied this corner site for many years and, externally at least, is largely unchanged in appearance.

This photograph of Manse Road, looking north towards Whitburn Cross, was taken around 1905 and shows, on the left, the private house at 14 Manse Road. Built in 1902 and largely unchanged externally today, the house was at one time occupied by Hugh Harper, whose haulage contractor's business was located on Manse Road. Immediately beyond, and with only a small portion of the roof gable visible, is the former Whitburn Register Office. Erected in 1888 by Whitburn Parochial Board, this was eventually sold in the early 1970s by the owners, West Lothian County Council. All of the other older properties seen here on the left-hand side of Manse Road nearer the Cross have since been demolished, including the house, offices and garage of Campbell Brothers (Coaches) Ltd. This company, which was in competition with James Browning, in 1921 operated the first bus service to run between Harthill and Bathgate. Four years later, having moved to Whitburn, the company inaugurated (and maintained until 1946) a service between Whitburn and Glasgow. All of the properties on the right of the picture have survived, their exteriors largely unchanged.

This photograph, taken in April 1928, shows some of the private houses on Armadale Road, and, further north on the hill, the former Tippethill Hospital. The first property on the left-hand side (part of whose frontage can be seen) is Ingleside. It was erected in 1903, and in 1928 was the residence of George F. Gillon, who ran a joinery business in Whitburn. While the single-storey properties seen here have largely survived, the double-storey blocks of miners' houses at Oakland and Viewfield Terraces have gone. These properties were owned by United Collieries Limited and, typically, had exterior staircases to their rear giving access to the upper storey. At the foot of Armadale Road, where the road bends sharply, are Almondbank Cottage and House, which at one time were used as a church and presbytery respectively. In May 1979, when a new chapel was opened at Croftmalloch by the Archbishop of St Andrews and Edinburgh, this chapel was closed. Today the chapel is lying disused but the presbytery alongside is now the offices of Felice Di Resta's Z Cars business.

The former Tippethill Fever Hospital, described on its opening as a 'magnificently appointed place', was built on higher ground almost equidistant between Armadale and Whitburn. Opened on 30 November 1901 at a cost of £8,836, it was initially run by a Joint Hospital Board made up of representatives from Bathgate, Whitburn and Armadale. Around 1902, following a widespread outbreak of smallpox, a smallpox pavilion was added, and after the eradication of the disease the pavilion was reused as a sanatorium for patients in the first stages of consumption. Although the hospital was extended on several occasions, by the early 1950s changing attitudes to health care led to a debate about its future role. The outcome of the debate was that the hospital should be closed and replaced with a new £2.3 million community hospital and £80,000 Sensory Resource Unit. On 28 March 2001 the now renamed Tippethill House was opened by the Scottish Health Minister Susan Deacon.

The official opening of Whitburn's new public park by its benefactor, Sir Adrian Baillie, was held on 22 September 1922, to coincide with the start of the annual Whitburn Children's Gala Day. From then, and until the new King George V Playing Field was opened in Baillie Street, the Children's Gala Day was held here. In 1967 the Gala Day festivities were extended over eight days and they became known as Whitburn Downdie Week and Gala Day. There are several suggested origins of the name Downdie, which applies only to natives of Whitburn. One explanation put forward is that the name Downdie referred to the 'down' or fibres that attached themselves to the clothing of the local weavers in days gone by. Another is that the name was applied to any person who 'downed the water' from the Whitburn Reservoir. A possible third explanation is that it came about when a homeless man called Downdie from nearby Livingston took up temporary residence in Whitburn and, unable to fend for himself, had to be cared for at the expense of the town.

On Sunday, 16 October 1921, this striking 17-foot-high war memorial was unveiled by General Sir Francis Davies. Located just inside the entrance to the public park, it was designed and erected by Roberts & Son, a Bathgate firm of sculptors. Paid for largely through public subscription, the memorial is a four-sided pedestal of rough Rubislaw granite, with four panels, each engraved with the names of local men who fell in the First World War. Atop the pedestal itself is the figure of a soldier standing with reversed arms. Among the assembled company at the unveiling were approximately 70 ex-servicemen who, together with other dignitaries, had marched four abreast from the Town Hall. Music was provided by the Bathgate Public Band and the East Whitburn Pipe Band. In May 1975 a new community centre was opened on the open space to the rear of the monument.

The historic Whitburn United Presbyterian Church (now the Parish Church) on Manse Road dates from around 1729 and is Whitburn's only listed building. In its original form the church was built with three lairds' lofts, one of which was reserved for the Baillie family, whose family vault is located here. Within the graveyard is a white-painted cast iron memorial slab to the memory of Elizabeth Paton, the illegitimate daughter of the poet Robert Burns and Betty Paton. In 1929, when the United Presbyterian Church rejoined the Church of Scotland, the church was renamed Whitburn South Parish Church. In 1930 the church was partially restored by the Baillie family at a cost of £1,300, when the lairds' lofts were removed and a new vestry and porch added. Unfortunately, in December 1955 a massive fire destroyed much of the church – only the outside walls and porch survived. Following a four-year restoration project costing £21,000, the church was re-dedicated in November 1959.

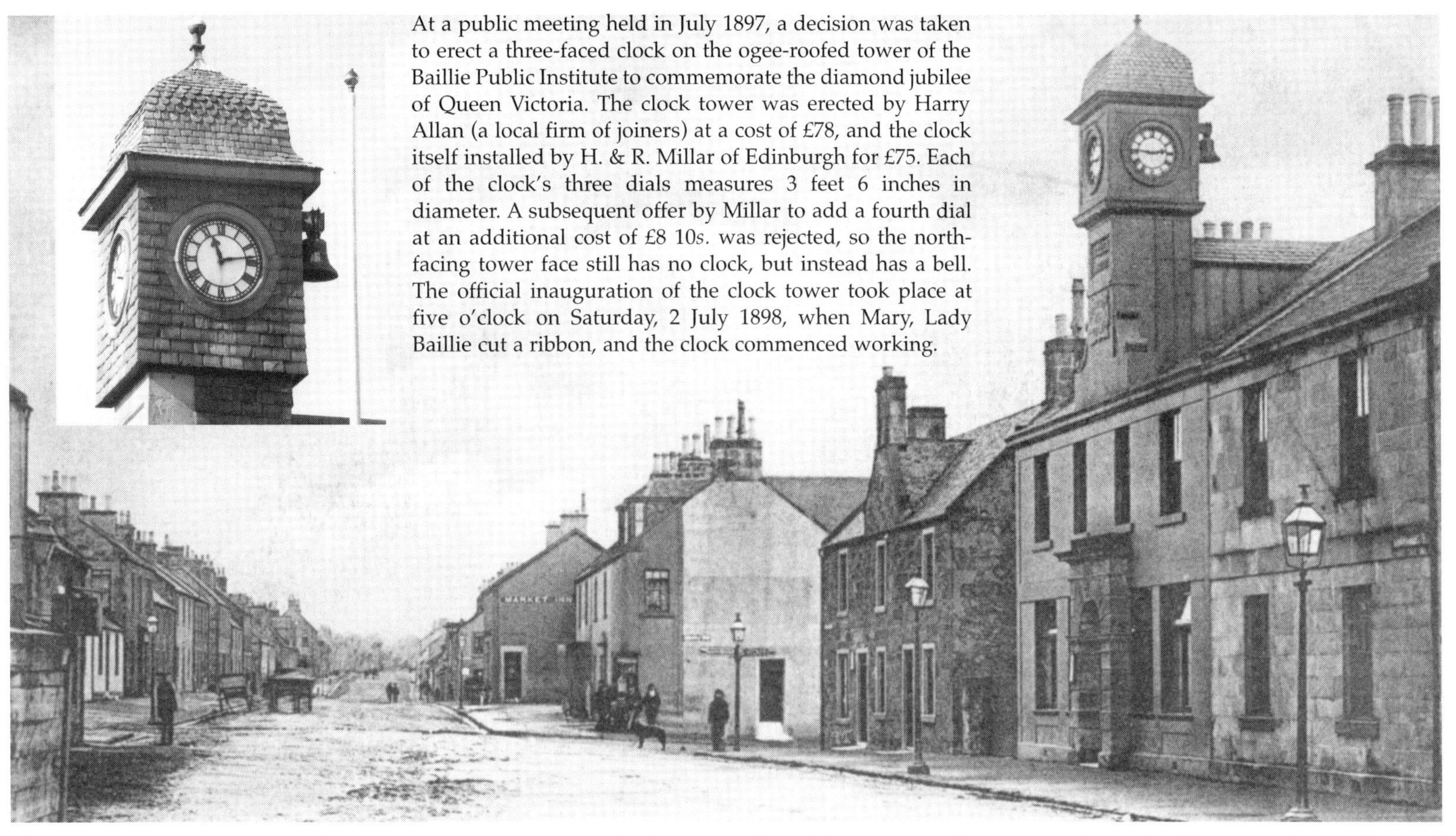

At a public meeting held in July 1897, a decision was taken to erect a three-faced clock on the ogee-roofed tower of the Baillie Public Institute to commemorate the diamond jubilee of Queen Victoria. The clock tower was erected by Harry Allan (a local firm of joiners) at a cost of £78, and the clock itself installed by H. & R. Millar of Edinburgh for £75. Each of the clock's three dials measures 3 feet 6 inches in diameter. A subsequent offer by Millar to add a fourth dial at an additional cost of £8 10*s*. was rejected, so the north-facing tower face still has no clock, but instead has a bell. The official inauguration of the clock tower took place at five o'clock on Saturday, 2 July 1898, when Mary, Lady Baillie cut a ribbon, and the clock commenced working.

The most striking building in Whitburn's East Main Street is the former Baillie Public Institute. This grey sandstone building, complete with its red sandstone baroque entrance porch, was opened in January 1879 and was one of five such institutes gifted to West Lothian communities by the Baillies of Polkemmet. Equipped as a coffee house and recreation centre, it included a library, reading room, games room and bowling hall. There was also living accommodation for the manager of the institute and for visitors. At a public meeting held on 5 February 1896, the institute was officially handed over to the community by Mary, Lady Baillie. Thereafter it was run by a local committee of councillors and ratepayers. From 1882 onwards, the institute was also used by the town council for their meetings and they eventually bought it over in 1959 for use as the Burgh Chambers. It continued to be used as such until local government reorganisation in 1975. Now the building houses the offices of West Lothian Council's Information Services and of the Registrar of Births, Marriages and Deaths.

One of Whitburn's best-known businesses, James Browning's bus and coach hire company and funeral director's, was established around 1900. James began his business by hiring out horses, which he stabled at the Old Market Inn on West Main Street. Later, when he moved into motor transport, he acquired the first Ford motor car in the county, causing much excitement locally. Browning later expanded into bus transport, operating routes between Armadale, Bathgate and Whitburn. In the early days, the buses were designed in such a way as to fulfil a dual role, in that the seats could be removed and the vehicle could then be used as a hearse. In this view one of the early hearses can be seen outside Browning's premises on East Main Street. In August 1993 the business was transferred to new offices on Longridge Road, where it operates to this day.

This late 1920s view is of the north side of East Main Street. In the main, the properties seen here (up to the tall building with the dormer windows in the middle distance) have survived. Over the years, these have housed some of Whitburn's best-known businesses. The building at the north-east corner of the Cross, for example (with the wall-mounted advertisement for 'Fry's delicious chocolates'), is Agnes and Jeannie Marshall's fruit shop. The small single-storey building beyond the Baillie Public Institute is the masonic lodge, while the two-storey building adjoining it is John Bowie's shoe shop. Beyond Bowie's, and totally hidden by the bus, are two single-storey whitewashed cottages, which were in 1929 the house and shop of Hugh Dewar, a local grocer. Further down the road still, at 19 East Main Street, was Gordon Robertson's grocery shop. The single-deck bus seen outside the Baillie Institute is one of James Browning's local buses.

At one time, Giacinto Boni's Cross Café was undoubtedly one of the most popular businesses in the vicinity of Whitburn Cross. Both Giacinto and his wife, Maria Concetta di Felice, were born in Italy, but their families had emigrated to Scotland, settling in the Whitburn area. In time, Giacinto and Maria's daughter (also Maria) and her husband, Giustino Franchitti, took over the running of the café. Giustino, known locally as Geordie, was a well-liked local character and older inhabitants still recall him wheeling his ice cream cart around the town in the 1930s. A keen supporter of the local junior football team, Geordie was renowned for his steaming hot cups of Bovril, which he gave out free during half-time to local and visiting teams alike. Although the café was eventually demolished, it was replaced by the present Cross Café, which was built just to the rear of the original café.

Almost all of the properties seen here lining both sides of East Main Street, looking west towards Whitburn Cross, have been demolished since this photograph was taken. These include all the houses on the north side of the street up to the two-storey property alongside the delivery van. In their place, new flats have been erected. Among the properties seen in the photograph is William Lawson's Millbank Farm and dairy. The dairy (second building on the right), which was accessed from Main Street, supplied both fresh and sour milk (the latter known as 'soor dook'), which could be delivered or collected from the dairy itself. At one time, it was common practice for children in the household to be given the chore of collecting milk from the dairy in a milk-can or jug. Almost directly opposite the diary was the former Whitburn Free Church. Opened in 1857, the church was later renamed Brucefield Church, in memory of the Rev. Bruce, a former minister. In 1966 a new church (also named Brucefield) was built alongside the original church, which then became the church hall.

Above: Undoubtedly, the longest continuously operating business in Whitburn is Kenneth and Norman Livingston's butcher's shop in East Main Street. When first opened around 1887, this shop was owned by a Robert Meek. On his retirement in 1924, the shop was taken over by his son, also Robert, who ran it until 1948. As well as being a butcher, Robert Junior was also one-time winner of Edinburgh's prestigious Powderhall Sprint. In 1948 the shop was taken over by another butcher, John Livingston, who is seen here in the 1950s alongside his delivery van, which is parked to the rear of the shop. On John's death in 1972 the shop was taken over by his sons who, in the best family tradition, carry on the business to this day.

Below: Perhaps the most serious rival to James Wood & Sons' long-established Yetthouse Bakery was the equally well-known family business of A. & C. Fisher. This business was started by Robert Fisher in 1929, with one shop on the south side of West Main Street, at the corner of Union Road. Later, when sons Alexander and Colin came into the business, it became Robert Fisher & Sons. At this time a second shop selling fruit was opened alongside the baker's shop, and delivery vans (similar to the one seen here in this 1930s photograph) were put on the road. Around 1975, when the section of West Main Street near the Cross was being redeveloped, the business moved to the opposite side of the street, latterly into the former Commercial Bank of Scotland building, which at the time had been lying empty for a few years. Today the business is run by the founder's grandsons, Alister and Norman.

The dimensions of this large boulder (known locally as the Eppie Stone) on the upper reaches of the White Burn can easily be gauged from early photographs, which show as many as eleven people either standing or sitting on it. Despite the belief that a local witch was buried here, it was a popular venue for picnickers and local youths, who would use the boulder as a launching pad for their games of 'jump the burn'. While the jump was not too strenuous, any misjudgement would leave the unhappy young person requiring a good scrub when he or she returned home, as the 'washings' from the nearby Polkemmet Colliery entered the burn further up and dirtied the water. As for the origin of the Eppie Stone, it has been suggested that it takes its name from Eppie Gray, the daughter of a local shepherd, who was murdered when she refused her lover's offer of marriage.

In 1816 James Wilson, a wealthy Whitburn merchant, left a sum of money to provide a school specifically for 'the labouring poor' of Whitburn. Built on a greenfield site beyond East Main Street, the James Wilson Endowed School comprises the taller portion of the Whitburn Public School building, seen here immediately to the left of the tall pole. At that time, the school was one of three local schools, the others being the Lady Baillie School and the Parish Church School. In the 1870s the James Wilson Endowed School was taken over by the newly appointed Torphichen School Board and thereafter was extended on several occasions. Latterly, in 1967, a new school (Whitedale Primary School) was built to the rear of the building, and the public school was used as an annexe to the new school. The annexe was closed about twelve years ago and is currently boarded up awaiting demolition. New housing is to be built on the site.

This Whitburn Public School photograph – regrettably undated but probably taken in the early 1900s – shows a class posing outside the school for their annual photograph. Although there was at that time a prescribed school uniform of navy and white, it would appear from this photo that the wearing of it was not strictly enforced! At the age of eleven or twelve years, these pupils would have been separated according to their academic ability, and the more academically inclined pupils would attend Bathgate Academy, while the others would transfer to Lindsay High School (also in Bathgate), where their curriculum would largely consist of commercial and technical subjects. Today local children no longer have to travel to Bathgate for secondary schooling but instead can attend Whitburn Academy, which was opened on West Main Street in 1967.

In 1846 a station known as Whitburn (but in fact situated in East Whitburn) was opened on the North British Railway's Bathgate, Wilsontown, Morningside and Coltness line. Although primarily intended to serve the local collieries along the line, it was also used to provide a rudimentary passenger service. With the gradual closure of local collieries, traffic on the line declined and finally, in May 1930, all of the stations on the line were closed to passenger traffic, although goods traffic continued to use the line until 1962. By the late 1960s the Stationmaster's House, seen here to the rear of the ticket office and waiting room, was lying derelict. Although it was reconstructed in the 1970s, it was later demolished. Initially the track was lifted only as far as East Whitburn Mains Farm, but in the end the entire line was taken away.

A little to the south of Whitburn Station, a freight line branched off to the east to serve the Whitrigg Fireclay Mine and the Whitrigg Colliery. The latter, also known as the Lady Colliery in honour of Lady Baillie of Polkemmet, was formally opened on 24 March 1908 and was operated by Messrs Hugh and Robert Forrester. Although it had been intended that the first sod would be dug by Lady Baillie herself, this honour in fact fell to the wife of one of the owners when inclement weather prevented Lady Baillie from carrying out the ceremony. The pit continued to be operated by the Forresters until the nationalisation of the coal industry in 1947, when it passed into the hands of the National Coal Board. At its peak, the colliery employed approximately 1,300 men and produced 1,600 tons of coal per day. It ceased production in 1972.

Our Lady of Lourdes Church, seen here in April 1929, was one of the most prominent buildings on West Main Street, Blackburn. Before its official opening by Bishop Henry Grey Graham in June 1924, services had been conducted in a variety of local venues. These included a building that later became a masonic lodge, and a picture hall. The new church was built with a hall at ground level and the actual church above, the latter being accessed by a set of steep steps. On the evening of 9 March 1954, the church was destroyed in a major fire, and thereafter (until October 1961, when a second church was built on the Bathgate Road) services were held in the local Miners' Welfare Hall. Both sides of the street (as far as Blackburn Cross in the distance) are lined with single-storey cottages. While those on the south side of the street have largely survived, their counterparts on the north side (with the notable exception of St Margaret's Cottages) have been demolished.

In this late 1920s view of West Main Street, Blackburn, just to the west of the Cross, the north side of the street is largely taken up by the Blackburn Baillie Institute (on the far left) and Alexander Ferguson's Turf Hotel. The institute, which was modelled on the Fauldhouse Baillie Institute, was formally opened in December 1911, and was equipped with recreation rooms, a kitchen and (with the needs of the miners in mind) two public baths on the ground floor. On the upper floor were a library and reading rooms, and accommodation for the resident caretaker. Initially run as a temperance establishment by a local management committee, the institute was taken over in 1933 by the local Miners' Welfare Committee. They renovated it and enlarged it by building a hall at the rear. By the 1970s competition from other local venues saw use of the institute fall dramatically and, as a consequence, both the institute and hall were demolished. Today, new housing at Quoiter's Court stands on the institute site.

In the 1920s, following the passing of the 1919 Addison Act, the first council houses in Blackburn were built on greenfield sites to the north of the town on the Bathgate Road. The first of these new council houses, seen here on the right of the picture at Riddochhill, were two- and three-apartment houses and were built over a period of twenty years. After 1945 a second major council housing scheme was begun on the opposite side of Bathgate Road, at Murrayfield, first to house an influx of miners seeking work in the local pits and later to accommodate Glasgow 'overspill' – the latter attracted to the area by the prospect of work at the new British Motor Corporation truck and tractor factory in Bathgate.

Until the wholesale demolition of the older properties on West and East Main Street in the 1930s, the area around Blackburn Cross was the commercial heart of the community. In addition to the Turf Hotel, the Almond Inn and the Crown Inn, there was a bank, a branch of the West Calder Co-operative Society, Josephine Ezzi's newsagent's shop, a picture house, and several grocers' and newsagents' shops. Within Wallace's Buildings (far left) on the north-east corner of the Cross, was John Johnston's grocery and wine merchant's shop. Immediately beyond Stark's Buildings (easily recognisable by its fancy roof-mounted ironwork) was the Co-operative store. On the opposite side of Main Street is Albert Buildings (far right), occupied by Joseph Galloway's confectionery shop and George Anderson's motor and cycle shop. Also on this side of the street were McInally's grocery and the Paton Brothers' popular Picture Palace. The latter was one of two picture houses owned by the Paton family, the other being located at nearby Stoneyburn.

In common with other West Lothian communities, on 22 June 1911 Blackburn marked the Coronation of King George V and Queen Mary with a day of celebrations. The day began with the marshalling of local children in the playground of Blackburn Public School and then the 400 children, headed by two pipers, marched along Main Street to a field at Riddochhill, where each child was given refreshments and an enamelled mug decorated with the portraits of the King and Queen. Also in the parade, but seated in a horse-drawn carriage and flanked by a mounted escort, were two local residents, George Baird and Miss Bryce, who were 'King' and 'Queen' for the day. An article in the local newspaper at the time noted the presence of a 'number of youths in strange apparel' – perhaps they included some of the oddly dressed characters seen here who were participating in the cycle parade!

Blackburn's first Children's Gala Day was held in July 1912, utilising funds left over from the previous year's Coronation Day celebrations. For this first Gala Day, the children assembled in the school playground before parading along Main Street to Riddochhill Farm, where games, races and a football competition were held. Later tea and pastries were given to each child. This picture shows the Gala Day procession in 1913. The Gala Day was interrupted by the First World War, but with the exception of two further brief interruptions in 1921 and 1988 caused, respectively, by a national miners' strike and a lack of volunteers, it has continued to this day.

From about 1891 until 1908, when a new purpose-built church was opened on East Main Street, the congregation of Blackburn United Free Church worshipped in the local village hall. Their new church, seen here in April 1929, was officially opened on 21 June 1908. It was designed in the Gothic style by Messrs W. Roberts and Sons of Bathgate. In 1936 a Bathgate minister, the Rev. John Lindsay, and his wife bought the village hall that had served as a temporary church for almost twenty years and gifted it back to the congregation. In early 1974 this hall (renamed the Lindsay Hall in memory of this minister) was sold by the congregation for use as a masonic lodge. All of the buildings seen here (including the manse and the single-storey Woodlands Cottage) have survived to this day and are, externally at least, little changed.